hair
accessories

hair
accessories

by Sarah Drew

THE GUILD OF MASTER CRAFTSMAN

PUBLICATIONS

First published 2012 by
Guild of Master Craftsman Publications Ltd
Castle Place, 166 High Street, Lewes,
East Sussex BN7 1XU

Text and illustrations © Sarah Drew, 2012
Copyright in the Work © GMC Publications Ltd, 2012

ISBN 978-1-86108-879-6

Set in King and Myriad
Colour origination by GMC Reprographics
Printed and bound by Hung Hing Printing
Co. Ltd.

Publisher Jonathan Bailey
Production Manager Jim Bulley
Managing Editor Gerrie Purcell
Senior Project Editor Wendy McAngus
Editor Judith Chamberlain-Webber
Managing Art Editor Gilda Pacitti
Designer Robert Janes
Cover photo Rebecca Mothersole
Photographer Andrew Perris

contents

Continued...

BUTTON

CUBIST

FANTASTIC

MERMAID

SWEETIE

ROSE

FLORA

CLARA

The Projects

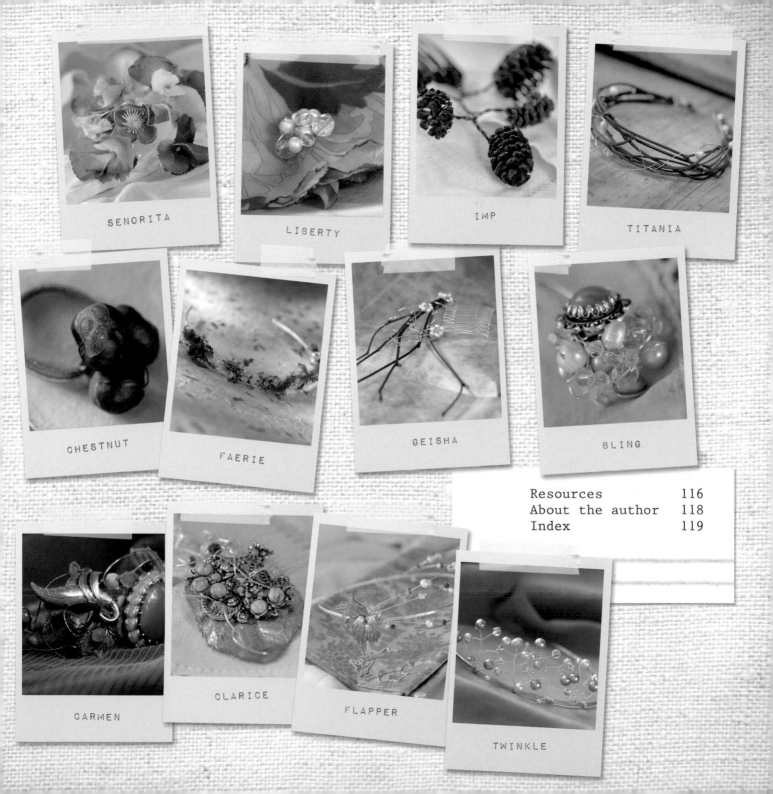

SENORITA

LIBERTY

IMP

TITANIA

CHESTNUT

FAERIE

GEISHA

BLING

CARMEN

CLARICE

FLAPPER

TWINKLE

Tools and materials

THE TOOLS YOU'LL NEED TO MAKE YOUR HAIR ACCESSORIES ARE MAINLY EVERYDAY ITEMS YOU SHOULD BE ABLE TO FIND AT HOME. MANY OF THE MATERIALS ARE JUST WAITING TO BE FOUND AT THE BACK OF DRAWERS OR AT YOUR FEET WHEN YOU GO OUT WALKING!

pliers and scissors

You've probably already got scissors suitable to use for these projects: sewing, household and nail ones are all fine. You may well have pliers and snips too, but if not you can buy them cheaply at hardware stores.

FLAT-NOSE PLIERS

Flat-nose pliers are the most useful for wirework. I like the ones with grips on the flat part but be careful not to overwork the wire with them as they can easily mark it and take any plating off.

WIRE SNIPS

These are also called cutters, depending on where you buy them, and are another essential. I like the side cutters best as you can get in really close to the wire for a nice neat cut.

SMALL SCISSORS

Little nail scissors or embroidery scissors are perfect for trimming lace, fabric or flower edges to create the shape you're after.

FABRIC SCISSORS

Some sharp fabric scissors are good to get a clean edge when cutting out petal shapes or ribbon.

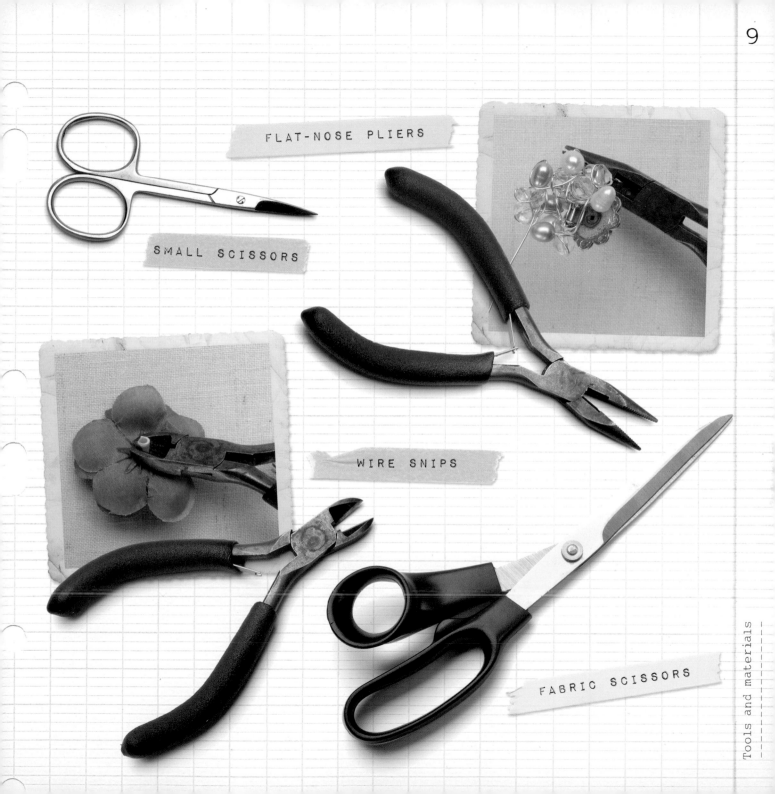

FLAT-NOSE PLIERS

SMALL SCISSORS

WIRE SNIPS

FABRIC SCISSORS

other tools and gadgets

There are loads of craft gadgets you can buy, but some are more useful than others! A glue gun is handy and effective though and a rotary power tool has enough uses to make it a good investment.

CROCHET HOOKS

Crochet hooks are available from craft shops, markets or online. Different sizes will create different effects, depending on what look you prefer. A small hook (1–2.25mm:UK4–13:US10–B/1) will produce close, delicate work whereas a larger hook (3.25–4mm:UK10–8:USD/3–G/6) will produce more loopy open work. If you prefer knitting, then try knitting with wire for a very similar effect.

FILE

You can normally get small needle files at markets quite cheaply, but if you don't have one, a new nail file or emery board works just as well.

ROTARY POWER TOOL

This is needed if you want to drill unusual finds such as woodland seeds or children's building blocks. You'll probably have to tape down what you're drilling so it doesn't skid about. Alternatively you could use a hand-drill instead.

GLUE GUN

The hot glue gun sticks some surfaces much more effectively than superglue, especially fabric or shiny surfaces. Buy extra glue rods so you don't run out.

CROCHET HOOK

FILE

GLUE GUN

Model : Handy Glue Gun
100 - 240 Volts ~
13 Watts 50Hz

ROTARY POWER TOOL

RC250
160W, 230V ~ 50Hz
8,000 - 35,000 rpm
CE RoHS
Made in PRC

Tools and materials

household items and essentials

You've probably got most of these items lurking around the house somewhere. In fact, craft projects are probably the only things my iron gets used for! PVA glue and different-sized needles are always useful.

NEEDLES

Strong, sharp ones are the most useful for creating holes in flowers and other items to decorate your accessories.

IRON

A normal household iron is great for moulding decorations made with plastic bags.

NEEDLE

IRON

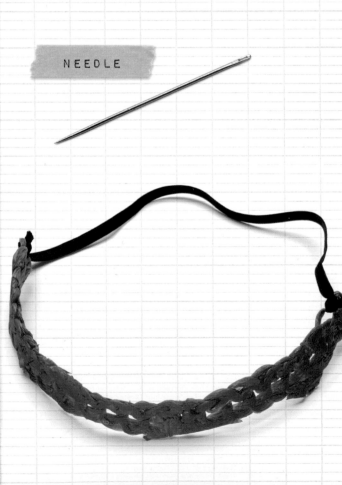

GLUES

Children's PVA glue is safe and easy to use so it's great for stiffening fabric, but it's also useful to have superglue and a glue gun for lots of different projects.

WIRE

The wire you use for these projects normally comes coiled in a plastic pack or on a reel. Try not to completely undo the wire circle when you take some off to use, because if the wire unravels it can get kinks in it.

The diameter of wire is measured using either millimetres, fractions of an inch, or specific wire gauges. Standard Wire Gauge (SWG) is the gauge generally used in the UK, with 0 being the largest and 50 the narrowest. American Wire Gauge (AWG) is the standardized wire gauge system used in the USA, with 0 being the largest and 40 the narrowest.

The main sizes that it's good to have to hand are 0.6mm (SWG 24, AWG 23) and 0.3mm (SWG 30, AWG 29) or 0.4mm (SWG 27, AWG 26). If you're working with bigger beads or stiffer fabrics and flowers, then 0.8mm (SWG 21, AWG 20) is sturdier to use.

I normally use silver-plated or gold-plated copper wire, but the coloured enamel wires look gorgeous too. Experiment with different colours for unusual effects.

GLUES

WIRE

hair basics

As you're spending all this time making embellishments, the bases you use should be as plain as possible to allow your creations to shine! Most items can be picked up cheaply from craft shops or jewellery findings websites.

CLIP SLIDES

You can use grips or snap-style slides. Have a think about how you want your design to look in your hair as they do become part of the overall effect.

HAIR COMBS

Clear or hair-coloured plastic combs are good if you don't want the comb itself to be a feature of the decoration, while metal ones make for a more visible vintage look. Department stores normally sell plain ones and they are widely available on the internet.

CLIP SLIDES

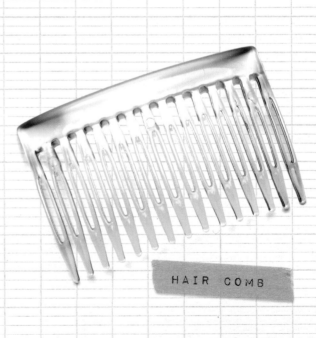

HAIR COMB

HAIR ELASTICS

You can choose plain elastics to hide in your hair or bright designs to work with the look that you're aiming for.

BARRETTE CLIPS

You can buy plain metal barrette bases from jewellery findings suppliers for you to decorate how you wish. Remove the middle spring to make it easier to attach your design to the front, then put it back into place at the end.

TIARA BASES

Plain flat metal bands are the most useful and easily available from craft shops or sites on the internet. Remember to bend the ends out before you start, so the base takes on a horseshoe shape, as this will make it a lot more comfortable to wear.

BARRETTE CLIP

HAIR ELASTICS

TIARA BASE

embellishments

You really can use whatever you like or whatever you have; as long as it can be crocheted, knitted, bent, threaded or drilled you can incorporate it into your hair accessories. Be as creative and crazy as you like!

NATURAL FOUND MATERIALS

Little cones, seeds and pods look lovely and unusual on tiaras and combs, as do shells and even holey pebbles. In an urban environment, look out for interesting bits of broken plastic or sweet wrappers. All sorts of things you find by your feet look lovely on hair accessories.

BUTTONS

New and vintage buttons work brilliantly in loads of different hair accessory designs. You've probably got some at home or have a look in second-hand markets.

BEADS

A lot of the projects don't need loads of beads so instead of buying them you can re-use ones you have already or give a new life to ones from a broken necklace. Vintage beads from antique shops, internet auction sites and second-hand markets are a good way to give your pieces a really unique look. There are some websites for bead shopping listed in the Resources section (see page 116) to tempt you too!

NATURAL FOUND MATERIALS

BEADS

BUTTONS

VINTAGE BROOCHES AND EARRINGS

It doesn't really matter if the brooches are missing a few stones – you can add extra beads to them and incorporate them into your designs for a lovely eclectic look. Designs with open work or holes in them are best for the projects in this book, as they're easier to wire into place.

FABRIC FLOWERS

If you're lucky you might be able to pick up some beautiful vintage silk flowers – snip them off old hats! Or try market stalls, department stores and garden centres to find new ones. Don't spend too much on them though as you'll be embellishing them further with sparkly beads.

FABRIC AND LACE

Vintage lace mats and tablecloths are great to snip up for hair decorations or you can cut up lace tops and dresses from second-hand shops. You can buy lace new, of course, but sometimes you're required to buy at least 20in (0.5m), which might be more than you need. Old head scarves and vintage skirts or blouses are an excellent source of fabrics that you can cut shapes from to make flower petals.

FABRIC FLOWERS

VINTAGE BROOCHES AND EARRINGS

FABRIC AND LACE

Techniques

HERE ARE SOME BASIC STRAIGHTFORWARD TECHNIQUES TO TRY. ONCE YOU'VE MASTERED THEM YOU WILL BE ABLE TO MAKE ALL THE PROJECTS IN THIS BOOK. YOU CAN COMBINE THEM WITHIN A DESIGN TO PRODUCE YOUR OWN UNIQUE CREATIONS.

twisting

This is a useful, flexible technique that can produce different looks depending on the thickness and colour of wire that you choose to use. The twisted branches it creates look lovely on a tiara or comb.

BE CAREFUL NOT TO TWIST THE WIRE TOO TIGHTLY AS IT CAN SNAP IF IT IS OVERWORKED.

TWISTING A WIRE TREE

1 Bend a 12in (30cm) length of 0.3mm (SWG 30, AWG 29) or 0.4mm (SWG 27, AWG 26) wire in half and thread on a bead up to the middle point. Cross the wire ends over each other.

2 Twist the bead so that the wires twist together for about ½ in (13mm). Take each of the wires out to the side ready to add more beads.

3 Thread a bead onto one of the wire ends and hold it about ½ in (13mm) from the first wire-twist before folding the wire over the bead and twisting as before until it meets the end of the first twist.

4 Do the same on the other side and twist the bead until the wire meets the centre point of the other two twisted branches.

5 Twist the two wires together to create a central trunk before adding more beads to the sides as before.

6 The shape will look more organic and natural if the side branches are not all level. After you've added the required number of beads, twist the two ends together to produce a stalk that you can use to attach the branch to combs, slides or tiara bases.

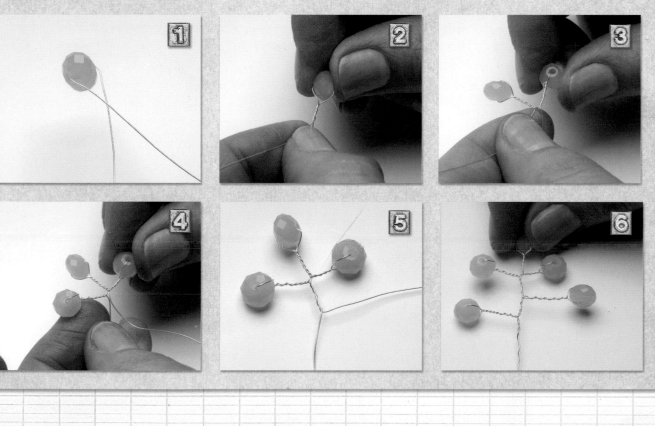

crocheting

If you can crochet with wool, you're a step ahead here.
Don't worry if you can't though because in some ways it's easier
to learn to crochet with wire as it stays put!

CROCHETING WITH WIRE

1   Cut 2ft (60cm) of 0.3mm (SWG 30, AWG 29) or 0.4mm (SWG 27, AWG 26) wire and make a loop at one end by wrapping an inch of the wire back round on itself.

2   Put your crochet hook through the loop from front to back.

3   Wrap the wire anti-clockwise round the hook above the first loop you made.

4   Pull the wire through the initial loop that was on the hook. You should just have one loop left on the hook now.

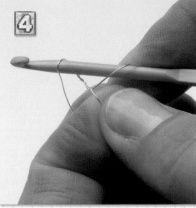

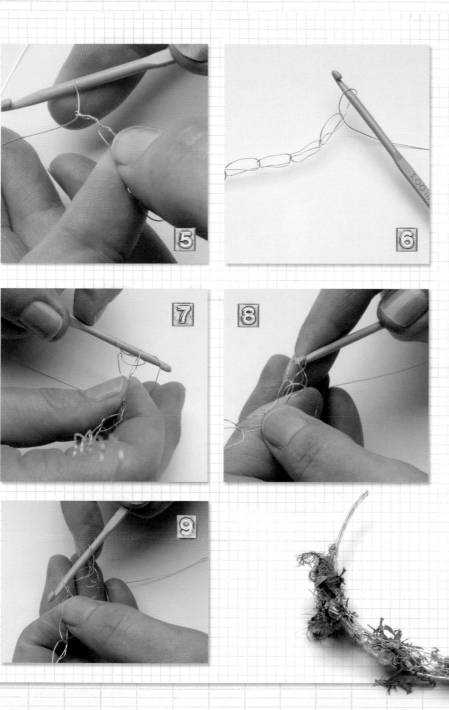

5 Bring the wire anti-clockwise round the hook again and pull it through the loop that is on the hook to make another 'chain' link.

6 Continue this process to create a whole row of linked loops as long as you need.

7 To start the second row, change direction and put the hook (with one loop still on) through the last link you created.

8 Bring the wire back round the hook anti-clockwise and pull it through both loops so just one is left on the hook.

9 Work your way along the whole length of chain in the same way until you reach the other end.

half-wrapping

This is a pretty Art-Nouveau style of wirework that's practical too as it holds the beads in place without having to use glue. Experiment with where you place the beads to create lovely berry-like tendrils to incorporate into tiaras and combs for a natural look.

HALF-WRAPPING BEADS

1 Thread your chosen bead onto a length of 0.6mm (SWG 24, AWG 23) wire and hold it where you'd like it to sit.

2 Take the wire half way round the bead to the other hole so that the bead is half-wrapped.

3 Using your thumb and forefinger, smooth out a nice curve in the wire next to the bead for about 1in (2.5cm).

4 Add another bead, secure with a half-wrap as before, and carry on.

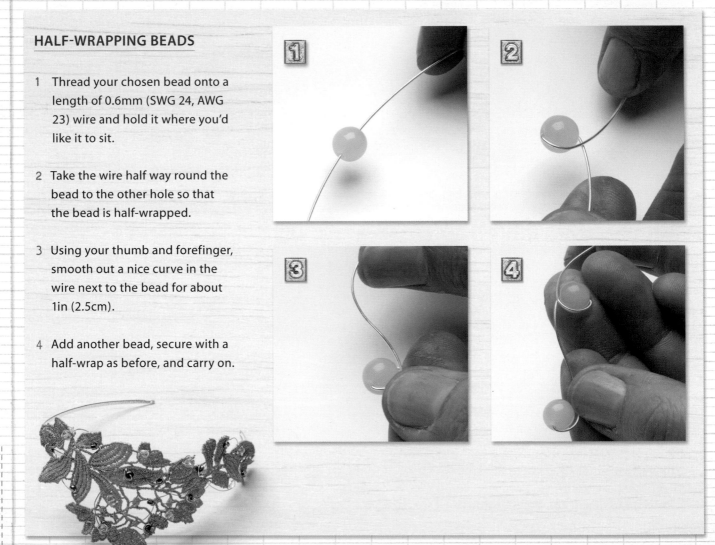

stiffening fabric

Stiffening lace and fabric with PVA glue makes them much easier to work with especially if you're weaving wire in and out of them. It also means your accessories will hold their shape and last much longer.

STIFFENING LACE

1 Put a blob of PVA glue about the size of a cherry tomato in a rectangular plastic container about 6 x 3in (15 x 7.5cm) (one that you don't need for food!).

2 Add around 2 tablespoons of warm water and mix together using your fingers until the glue dissolves.

3 Put your piece of material in the mixture so that it is fully immersed and soaked right through with the glue.

4 Carefully take the lace out of the container, squeezing out a little bit of the excess mixture (so you can see the lace holes again).

5 Put the lace piece on a plastic bag to dry overnight (it won't stick to the plastic).

attaching flowers

Most of the projects covered in this book could have flowers incorporated into them, so if you get the hang of attaching them with wire it should be no trouble to have everything coming up roses!

FOR FLOWERS WITH A HOLE THROUGH THE MIDDLE

1 Trim the plastic back of the flower closer to the petals using your snips or little sharp scissors.

2 Thread a 6in (15cm) length of 0.4mm (SWG 27, AWG 26) wire through the centre hole from back to front, leaving about 2in (5cm) of wire at the back of the flower.

3 Choose a focal bead to sit in the centre of the flower and thread it onto the wire at the front of the flower.

4 Take this end of the wire back through to the back of the flower.

5 Twist the two ends of the wires together to create a twisted stalk which you can use to attach the flower to your design.

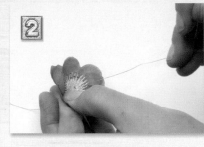

FOR FLOWERS WITHOUT A HOLE THROUGH THE MIDDLE

1. Use a strong, sharp needle to make a hole horizontally through the plastic back of the flower.

2. Thread a 6in (15cm) length of 0.4mm (SWG 27, AWG 26) wire through the hole you've made so that the flower sits at the middle point of the wire.

3. Cross the two ends of wire over each other and then carefully twist them together to create a twisted stalk.

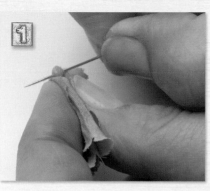
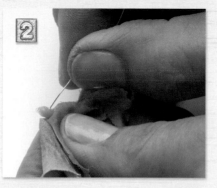

ribbon wrapping

Sometimes a metal tiara band can look a bit harsh or the wires wrapped round a comb can look messy. Wrapping organza ribbon (in a colour that tones with your hair) round it can soften the whole look and concentrate the eye on your design. It will make it a bit more comfortable to wear too.

WRAPPING A TIARA BASE

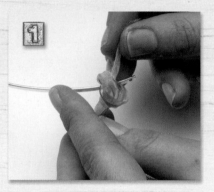  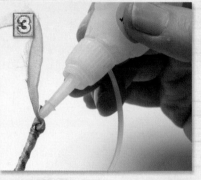

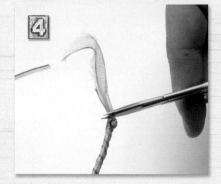

1　Cut 18in (46cm) of organza ribbon in a colour that tones in with your hair colour. Tie a knot around the end of a tiara base 1in (2.5cm) from one end of the ribbon.

2　Start wrapping the ribbon round the tiara base as tightly as you can, overlapping the ribbon so that none of the metal of the band shows through.

3　Wrap it right across the band to the other end, weaving it in and out of your design so that the metal band is completely covered. Tie the ribbon in a tight double knot at the other end of the band and seal each knot with a small blob of superglue.

4　Neatly snip off the end of the ribbon with small sharp scissors as close to the knot as possible.

finishing off

It might seem boring but finishing off your work neatly is quite important so your designs will look tidy and won't scratch you when you put them on! Practise wrapping the wire as tight as you can for a professional finish.

TIDYING THE WIRE ENDS

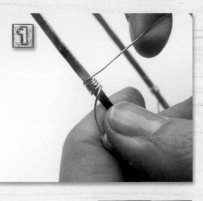
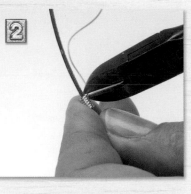

1   When you've completed your design, wrap the wire three times around the tiara base, comb or slide: keep it as close together and tight to the base as you can.

2   Using the flat side of your snips, cut the wire closely: try and cut it half way down the depth of the base or at the back of the slide to avoid sharp ends on the edge.

3   Squeeze the wrapped end flat to the base/comb/slide with your flat-nose pliers to make sure it's really snug.

4   Feel with your fingers to see if the end still feels sharp: if it does, just gently file the end with a needle or nail file. Be careful though as you can file silver- or gold-plating off quite easily.

button

Pretty vintage buttons
make a cute decoration
for a clip slide.

Everything you will need...

This is a simple way to use any beautiful spare buttons you have collected over the years. Or if you don't have a button hoard you could cut pretty ones off old clothes.

1 Large button

2 Small button

3 Clip slide

Glue gun

Sharp nail scissors

Assembling button

1 Choose two buttons that fit on top of each other nicely and in a colour combination you like.

2 Switch on your glue gun and insert the glue stick. It takes about five minutes to get properly warm.

3 Put a small blob of glue on top of the bigger button, then quickly put the smaller button onto it. Don't press too heavily otherwise the glue will come up through the button holes.

4 Squeeze a small, pea-sized blob of glue onto the widest part of the clip slide and quickly position the largest button on top of it.

5 When the glue has completely cooled, just trim any messy bits off with sharp nail scissors and you're done – it's ready to keep that naughty fringe out of your face!

IF YOU DON'T HAVE A GLUE GUN YOU COULD USE EPOXY RESIN GLUE OR ANOTHER STRONG GLUE INSTEAD.

YOU COULD MAKE LOADS
OF DIFFERENT BUTTON
SLIDES TO ACCESSORIZE
A QUIRKY UP-DO.

cubist

Use toy blocks to build a hair
decoration that's far from square.

Everything you will need...

Make something bright and funky out of those pesky toy building blocks that get everywhere and really hurt when you stand on them.

1 5–7 x toy building blocks

2 About 12in (30cm) of 0.3mm or 0.4mm (SWG 30 or 27, AWG 29 or 26) silver-plated wire

3 Sturdy hair elastic (with metal join)

Glue gun

Sharp nail scissors

Masking tape (optional)

Small hand drill or rotary power tool with $\frac{1}{8}$in (3mm) drill bit

Wire snips

Flat-nose pliers

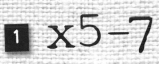

1 x5–7

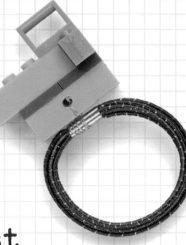

Assembling cubist

1 Work out how you want the building blocks to look: abstract sculpture looks good but don't make it too massive or precarious as it needs to be twisted around on the hair elastic.

2 Undo your arrangement. Switch on your glue gun and insert the glue stick. It takes about five minutes to get warm. Put small blobs of glue at the corner bumps of the bottom piece and gently clip the next ones onto it.

3 Let the glue cool and then repeat for your other row(s). Don't put on too much glue as you don't want it to ooze out everywhere.

4 Let the last layer of glue cool, then trim off any messy bits of glue with the nail scissors.

5 Using a small drill bit, drill a hole right through the side of the bottom brick of your arrangement.

6 Thread the wire through the hole. Wrap the wire around and thread through again twice to make the arrangement more sturdy.

7 Twist the block a few times so that the wire ends twist together for about 4in (10cm), then trim off any excess.

8 Place the metal join of the hair elastic under the blocks and wind the wire around it a few times.

9 Finish off by wrapping the wire around itself a couple of times just under the block arrangement, as you would when sewing on a button, to really strengthen it. Snip it with the wire cutters and squeeze the end in flush with the pliers (see page 27).

TAPE THE BLOCK ARRANGEMENT TO AN OLD PIECE OF BOARD WITH MASKING TAPE TO STOP IT SLIPPING AROUND WHEN YOU DRILL.

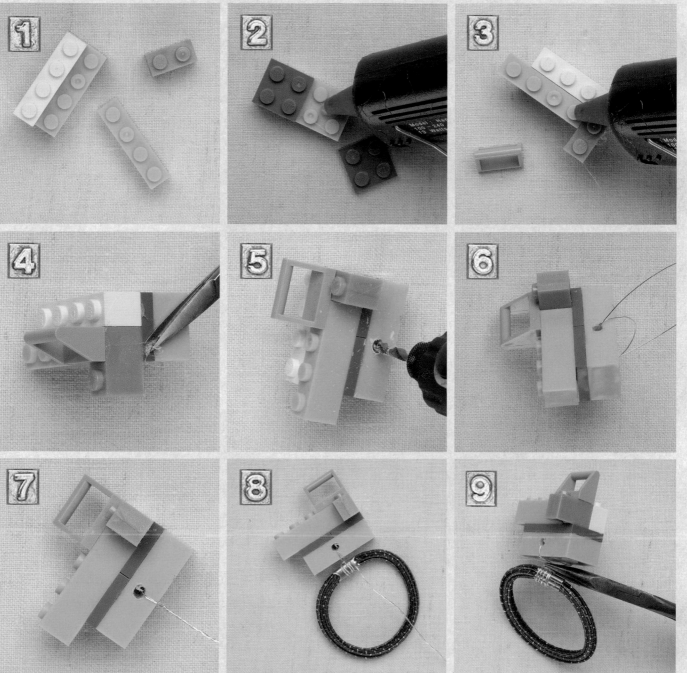

fantastic

Do everyone a favour
and turn ugly plastic
bags into something
lovely for your hair.

Everything you will need...

Thin plastic bags provide fantastic material that can be melted and formed into funky sculptural shapes to create bold, light headbands.

1 2 x coloured plastic bags

2 About 8in (20cm) of elastic

Sharp scissors

5mm (UK6: USH/8) crochet hook

Glass heat-proof bowl

Iron

Piece of clean paper

Superglue

1 x2

2

Assembling fantastic

1 Start cutting your plastic bags into strips about 2–4in (5–10cm) wide. It doesn't matter if they're not straight.

2 Double knot the pieces together to create a long continuous piece of plastic about 8¼ ft (2.5m) long.

3 At one end of the plastic, make a loop and secure it with a knot.

4 Put your crochet hook in the loop from front to back, bring the plastic around the hook anti-clockwise and pull it through the loop (see page 20).

5 Continue doing this until you have crocheted a chain of plastic about 12in (30cm) long.

6 Then go back along the other way, crocheting into the first chain; this is the second row, which will make the band wider. When you are finished, pull the end through the loop and tie in a knot.

7 Switch your iron on to a medium temperature with no steam. Put your plastic plait around a glass bowl about the size of your head. Put a clean piece of paper over the plastic, then carefully 'iron' it into a curved shape.

8 Peel the plait off the paper while it's still a bit warm so that the paper doesn't stick to it. Curve it round into a headband shape while it's still warm. Trim off any messy knot bits with your scissors.

9 Thread one end of the elastic through the last loop on the end of the band and tie a secure knot. Thread the other end of the elastic through the last loop of the other end of the plastic band and tie another secure knot. Finish off with a blob of glue on the knots before you snip off the tail end. The headband should now fit snugly on your head.

mermaid

If you've always wanted to be a
sea-bound temptress, now's your
chance to make a splash!

Everything you will need...

Any shells look good in this style and you always can buy them online if you can't get to the beach.

2

3

4

x10–15

---

1 7–12 x different-sized shells

2 Tiara base

3 3ft 3in (1m) of 0.6mm (SWG 24, AWG 23) silver-plated wire

4 10–15 x pearls

Small hand drill or rotary power tool with 1/8in (3mm) drill bit

Masking tape (optional)

Flat-nose pliers

Wire snips

Needle or nail file

1 x7–12

mermaid

MAKE SURE YOUR DRILL BIT IS NEW AND SHARP TO AVOID DAMAGING THE SHELLS OR COLLECT ONES THAT HAVE HOLES ALREADY SO YOU WON'T NEED TO DRILL THEM.

Assembling mermaid

1 Drill holes in any shells that don't already have holes. Take your time and do it gradually so they don't crack. Tape them down to a bench or other surface if they're slipping about.

2 Stretch out the ends of the tiara base so it's a horseshoe shape rather than circular. Wrap a 12in (30cm) length of wire three times around the base, about 2in (5cm) from one end.

3 Curve the wire out a bit with your thumb and attach a small shell or bead. Hold it in place with a half-wrap (see page 22). Wrap the wire once around the base.

4 Choose a bigger shell and hold it flat against the base. Thread the wire through the hole you drilled, then wrap the wire around the base again.

5 Work your way along the band, adding shells and pearls in this way until you are about two-thirds of the way along. Then wrap the wire three times around the base to secure it.

6 Work back the other way, filling in the gaps with shells and pearls as you go. Remember to tether the wire down on the base (or your own wirework) so that the design feels nice and sturdy. If you run out of wire, secure the end by wrapping it round the base. Then just add more wire by wrapping a new piece around the base a few times.

7 When you're happy with the shape and fullness of the shell cluster, wrap your wire around the base a few times. Cut off any excess wire with your snips. Check the headdress for sharp bits with your fingers and squeeze them in firmly with your pliers (see page 27). If they still feel sharp, just file them gently with the needle or nail file, and that's it, you're finished – you just need to find yourself a sailor to lure!

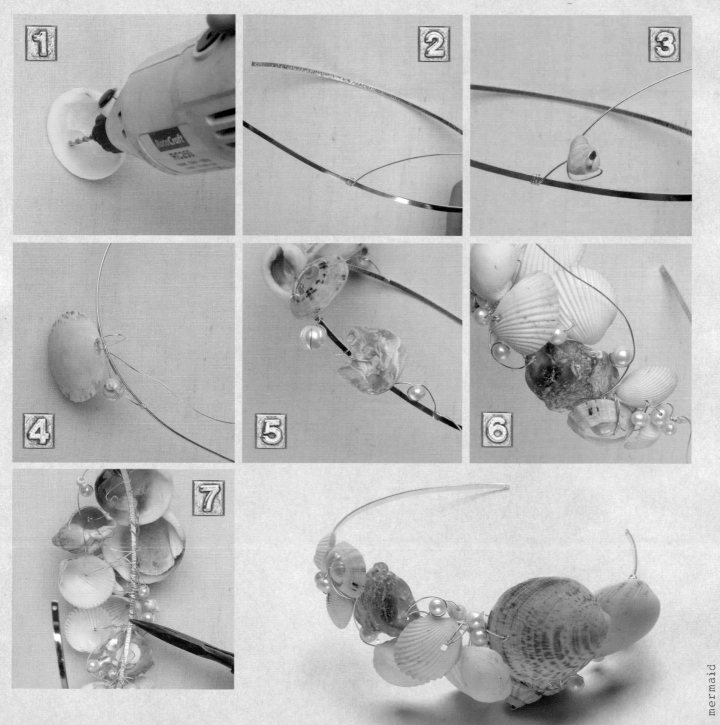

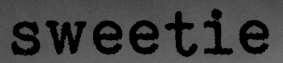

sweetie

Create a sweet look
with discarded
chocolate wrappers.

Everything you will need...

Using the foil wrappers from chocolates to make this quirky hair comb means there's no need to feel guilty about devouring them. You did it for art!

1

2

x10–15

3

1. 3ft (91cm) of 0.3mm or 0.4mm (SWG 30 or 27, AWG 29 or 26) dark-coloured wire

2. 10–15 x chocolates with different-coloured foil wrappers

3. Plain hair comb

Strong, sharp needle

Flat-nose pliers

Wire snips

sweetie

Assembling sweetie

1 Once you've eaten the chocolates, collect the foils together and carefully peel off any backing paper. It doesn't matter if the foils are crinkled.

2 Gently rip the foils into roughly square-shaped pieces, then roll them into tight balls so that the colour shows on the outside.

3 Pierce a hole through each ball with the needle so you can thread them onto the wire when you're ready.

4 Cut a 10in (25cm) length of wire, and thread on a smallish ball, pushing it to the middle point. Cross the ends of the wire over and gently twist the ball so that the wire ends twist together for about ½in (13mm).

5 Take one end of the wire out to the side to make a branch and thread another ball to about ½in (13mm) from the central point (see page 18). Cross the wire and twist back to the central trunk. Add about five to seven balls in this way and then twist the ends of the wire together for about 3in (7.5cm).

6 Make three branches like this. They can be different heights or have different numbers of balls to make them look more interesting.

7 Wrap the wire ends of the branches securely around the top band of the comb at regular intervals. Cut off the excess wire.

8 To finish off, check for sharp ends and squeeze them in with your pliers if necessary (see page 27), then fold all the branches back so that they sit above the comb teeth. This will make the comb less visible in your hair.

SCRUNCH THE BRANCHES UP ONCE THEY'RE ATTACHED TO THE COMB SO THAT THEY DON'T LOOK TOO REGULAR. DON'T TWIST THEM TOO TIGHT OR THEY MIGHT SNAP.

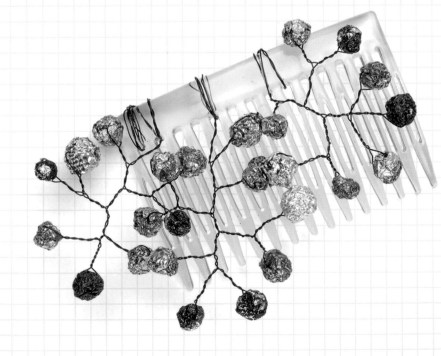

49

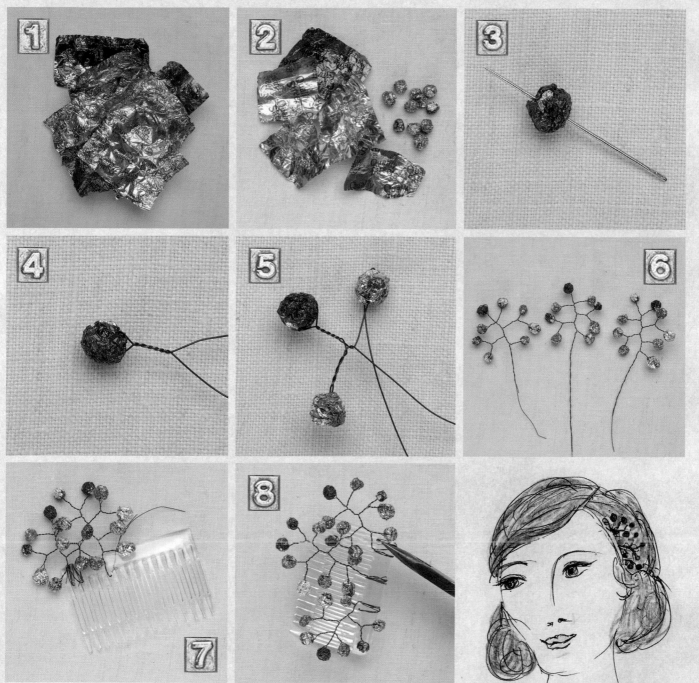

sweetie

fabric

rose

With this blooming gorgeous headdress, it's always summertime.

Everything you will need...

Once you've made this glorious headdress all you need to do is shimmy into a tea dress, get some crackly old records on and you're ready for a vintage afternoon tea party.

4 x4–5

5 x4–5

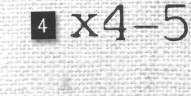

1. 12 x 6in (30 x 15.25cm) milliners' net
2. Tiara base
3. 12in (30cm) of 0.6mm (SWG 24, AWG 23) silver-plated wire
4. 4 or 5 x artificial roses
5. 4 or 5 x largish pearls or crystals

Small needle

Wire snips

Flat-nose pliers

Small file

Scissors

rose

Assembling rose

1 Gather the edge of the net together and place it on the tiara base how you'd like it to sit. I think it works well gathered above one eyebrow. Stretch out the ends of the base to make it more of a horseshoe shape. Wrap the length of wire three times around the base about 4in (10cm) from one end, then use the wire to 'stitch' the net into place over the base. Take care not to snag the net as you do this.

2 To attach flowers that have a hole through the centre, thread the wire through this hole, thread a pearl or crystal on and then loop the wire back down through the middle of the flower (see page 24). Wrap the wire back around the tiara base and through the net.

3 To attach flowers that have no holes through the centre, pull the stalks off and then use the needle to make a small hole through the plastic back of the rose (see page 25). Thread the wire attached to the tiara base through this hole and wrap the wire once around the base (and through the net) to hold it securely in place.

4 Once you have attached all the roses, cluster them carefully. I've used quite big ones here and packed them in tight for an exaggerated 1940s look.

5 Trim off the wire ends with your wire snips, flatten with the pliers and smooth down any rough edges with the file (see page 27).

6 Try your headdress on and decide how you'd like the net to sit. You'll probably need to trim it into a nice, curved shape so it sits prettily over your eye, and maybe just scrunch the flowers into place a little. That's it – get singing!

FOR A SLEEKER 1930S LOOK CHOOSE FLATTER FLOWERS SUCH AS ORCHIDS OR DAISIES SO THAT THEY SIT CLOSER TO YOUR HEAD.

IF THERE ARE ANY GAPS OR MESSY BITS COVER THEM
UP USING A LENGTH OF WIRE WITH HALF-WRAPPED PEARLS
OR BEADS (SEE PAGE 22) INCLUDED AT INTERVALS.

rose

flora

Romance is sure to blossom
when you wear this cute slide.

Everything you will need...

The twisted wire in the middle of this pretty hair slide makes the flowers look more real and delicate somehow. Select beads to match or tone with your outfit.

1. 7 x small beads
2. 12in (30cm) of 0.4mm (SWG 27, AWG 26) silver-plated wire
3. Smallish fabric flower
4. Clip slide

Wire snips

Flat-nose pliers

flora

Assembling flora

1 Thread your first bead onto the length of wire and push it up to the middle point, folding the wire in half over the bead.

2 Crossing the ends of the wire over each other, twist the bead so that the wires twist together for about $^3/_8$ in (1cm). Take each end of wire out to the sides.

3 Thread another bead onto one of the side wires, fold the wire over about $^3/_8$ in (1cm) from the middle trunk and twist the bead so the wire twists to meet the trunk central point (see page 18).

4 Thread a bead onto the other wire and repeat step 3, then twist both wires together for $^3/_8$ in (1cm). Add the rest of the beads on branches the same way. Twist the ends together for about 2in (5cm) to make a stem.

5 Trim the plastic back off the flower with your snips.

6 Thread the wire stem through the middle of the flower from front to back.

7 Hold the flower flat in front of the widest part of the slide, then 'stitch' the wire over the slide as firmly as you can. Use your pliers to pull the wires through tight and squash them down flat to the slide if needs be.

8 Wrap the wire around the back of the base of the flower (as you do when finishing sewing on a button) before trimming any excess off with your wire snips. And you're finished!

HOLD A BUTTON IN THE CENTRE OF THE FLOWER BEFORE YOU THREAD THE WIRE THROUGH FOR A BOLDER LOOK.

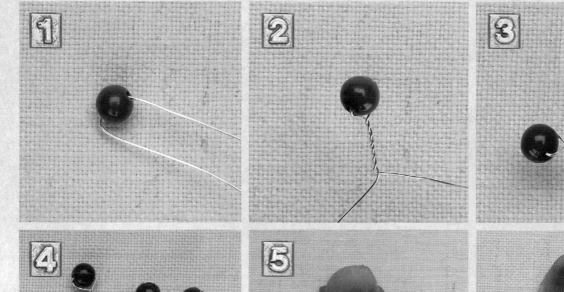

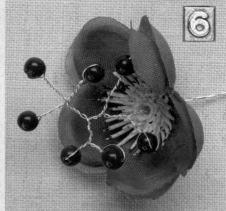

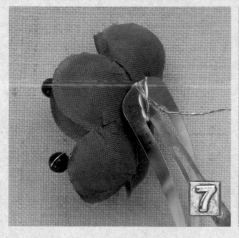

clara

This lace and bead
headdress is versatile
and stunning.

Everything you will need...

Different looks can be achieved just by changing your colour palette – ivory lace for sophisticated brides, black for a subtle evening headdress or neon pink for a funky party headband.

1 Piece of lace about 6 x 2in (15 x 5cm)

2 Tiara base

3 24in (61cm) of 0.6mm (SWG 24, AWG 23) silver-plated wire

4 30 x vintage pearls, diamante beads and crystals

PVA glue

Small scissors

Gold or silver paint spray (optional)

Flat-nose pliers

Wire snips

Needle or nail file

1

3

2

4 x30

clara

Assembling clara

1 Roughly cut out the piece of lace you want to use. We're aiming here for quite a 1930s asymmetric shape. Soak it in some watered-down PVA glue in a plastic container. Remove from glue and then let it dry out fully overnight on a plastic bag (see page 23).

2 Once it's dry, cut around your lace design carefully to neaten it up, using small scissors. If you'd like it gold or silver, spray it with paint as directed on the tin and leave to dry.

3 Bend the ends of the tiara out a bit to make more of a horseshoe shape, then cut a piece of wire about 12in (30cm) long and wrap this around the base three times, about 5cm (2in) from one end. Use the pliers to tighten it.

4 Next, thread the wire through one end of the lace, wrap the wire once around the base behind the lace and bring the wire back through to the front again.

5 Get a smooth curve to the wire by easing it with your thumb and forefinger, then thread on one of your beads. Hold it in place by snugly wrapping the wire around the bead in a half-wrap on top of the lace (see page 22).

6 Thread the wire through to the back of the lace, wrap it once around the base and then bring it back to the front again. Add another bead with a half-wrap and then repeat, adding beads as you work across the base until you reach the end of the lace.

7 Wrap the wire around the tiara base three times at the end, then work your way back across the lace adding more beads as you go. Try to keep most of the wirework behind the lace so it's nice and neat. When you run out of wire, wrap the end around the tiara base and then join another piece of the wire on to continue.

8 When you reach your starting point, wrap the wire around the base a few times and snip off any excess. Squeeze any sharp ends in with your pliers and file with the needle or nail file if necessary (see page 27), and you're finished!

YOU CAN ADD A BROOCH AS AN ASYMMETRIC FOCAL POINT. JUST PIN IT ON OR SNIP THE PIN OFF AND WIRE IT ON TO BE A MORE PERMANENT FIXTURE.

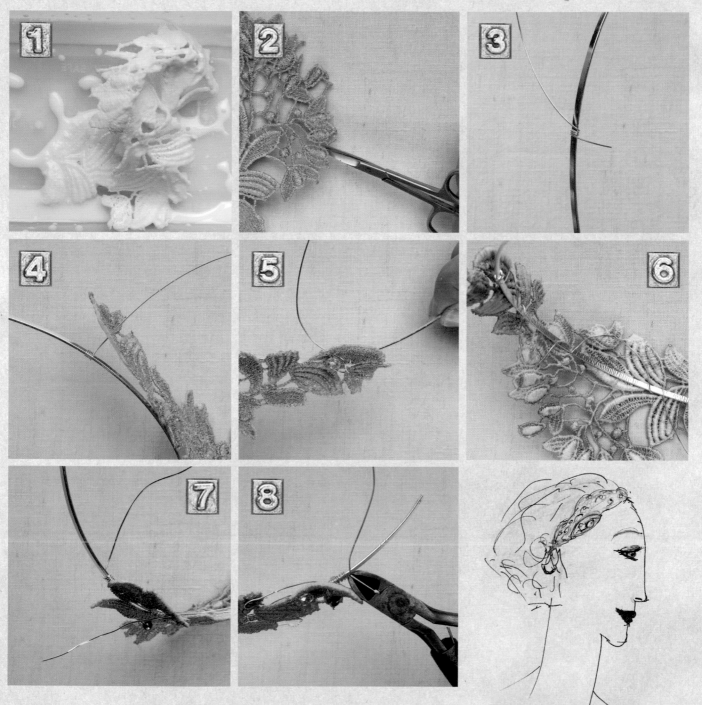

clara

senorita

Encase a bun with this adorable cage for a fresh, dressed-up look.

Everything you will need...

A lovely shiny bun makes the perfect background for this array of pretty flowers suspended on a delicate hair-cage.

1 10in (25cm) of 0.8mm (SWG 21, AWG 20) silver-plated wire

2 24in (61cm) of 0.6mm (SWG 24, AWG 23) silver-plated wire

3 10–15 x fabric flowers

4 15 x beads (pearls and crystals)

Flat-nose pliers

Wire snips

Needle or nail file

3 x10–15

1

4 x15

2

senorita

Assembling senorita

1 Gently bend the piece of 0.8mm wire round into a circle roughly 4in (10cm) in diameter, depending on how much hair is to be covered. Holding the loop with your pliers, wrap each end of wire three times around the opposite end to close the circle up. Snip any excess wire off and press the ends in with your pliers.

2 In the same place, attach 18in (46cm) of 0.6mm wire by wrapping it around the circle frame a couple of times.

3 Curve the wire with your thumb and forefinger, then thread on a bead until it's about 1in (2.5cm) from the circular frame. Hold the bead in place with a half-wrap (see page 22). Then smooth the wire into a nice curve again to continue.

4 If the flowers have a hole in the middle, thread the wire through that, add a bead and then pass the wire back through. If there is no central hole, make a hole in the plastic back with a needle so you can pass the wire through there (see page 24).

5 Once you've added a flower to the wire, follow it with a bead secured with a half-wrap about 1in (2.5cm) along. Continue adding flowers and beads along the wire for about 6in (15cm). You need to curve the wirework to create a bowl-like shape that will sit prettily over your bun.

6 Tether the wire on the other side of the circular frame by wrapping it around firmly a couple of times. Then go back across the frame in a different direction adding flowers and beads as you go.

7 Keep going in this way until you're happy with how many flowers and beads are attached and the fullness of the design. You'll need to add extra pieces of wire by wrapping them around the frame, and doing single wraps around the wirework to give the whole design its structure.

8 Trim any bits of wire off with your snips, squeeze the wire ends in with the pliers and file any rough edges with the nail or needle file (see page 27). Try the hair-cage on and squeeze it into shape a bit. You might need to use hair grips to hold it in place, depending on how shiny your bun is!

YOU COULD ADD DIFFERENT LENGTHS OF CHAIN TO THE WIREWORK AS YOU ADD THE FLOWERS. LOOP THEM IN OR LET THEM DANGLE A LITTLE.

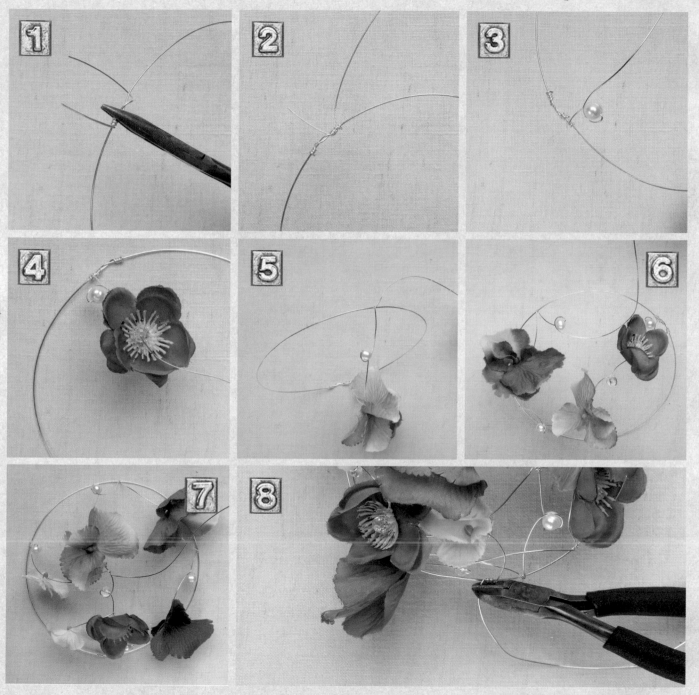

liberty

This fabulous flower
clip adds a touch of
bohemian style.

Everything you will need...

This soft flower clip is a great way to showcase pretty fabric scraps that you've been saving for years.

1

2

3 x9

4

1. 3 different co-ordinating fabric squares approximately 6 x 6in (15 x 15cm)

2. 18in (46cm) of 0.4mm (SWG 27, AWG 26) silver-plated wire

3. 9 x beads

4. Barrette clip

Paper

Pencil

Sharp scissors

Candle and matches or lighter

Flat-nose pliers

Wire snips

Needle

Assembling liberty

1 Draw a flower shape on paper about 4in (10cm) across with quite small petals (to make it look like a camellia) and cut it out.

2 Pin the flower to each different fabric and cut two of each out. Pile them up, alternating fabric types and trim the two top layers a bit smaller.

3 Carefully run the edge of each fabric flower through the candle flame to singe it. Some might curl up, which looks attractive (this is more likely with synthetic fabrics). Brush any black bits off with your fingers.

4 Take the wire and start making the bead cluster by threading a largish bead onto the wire until it's about 3in (7.5cm) from the other end. Thread the 3in (7.5cm) of wire through the layers of petals, then do a half-wrap around the bead to hold it in place (see page 22). Add another bead right next to it and do another half-wrap.

5 When you've added all the beads you want, take the wire through to the back, gather up the fabric a bit to make the petals sit in a 'cup' shape, then twist the two ends of wire together to form a stalk.

6 Take the centre arm out from the back of the barrette clip so that you can wrap the wire stalk around the main part of the clip more easily. Wrap it around as many times as you can on both sides of the stalk to steady it, then just carefully push the arm back into place. Snip off any ends of wire, squeeze to secure (see page 27) and you're finished!

MAKE THREE CONTRASTING FLOWERS TO CLUSTER ON A CLIP FOR A MORE DRAMATIC PIECE TO WEAR AT THE BACK OF AN UP-DO.

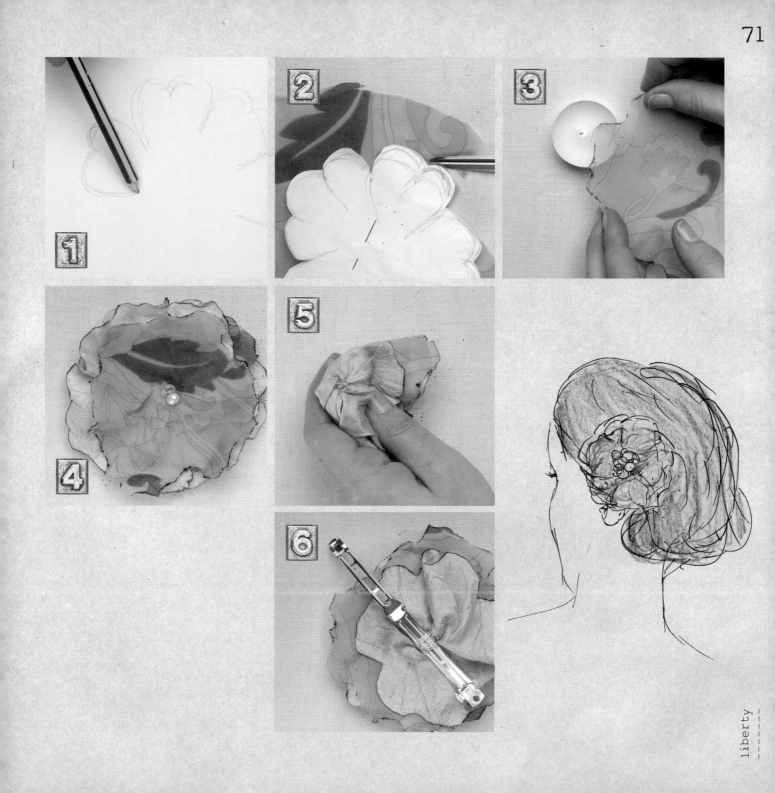

woodland

imp

Celebrate woodland
treasures with this
individual slide.

Everything you will need...

This is an excellent way to showcase natural treasures you've discovered on walks in the woods.

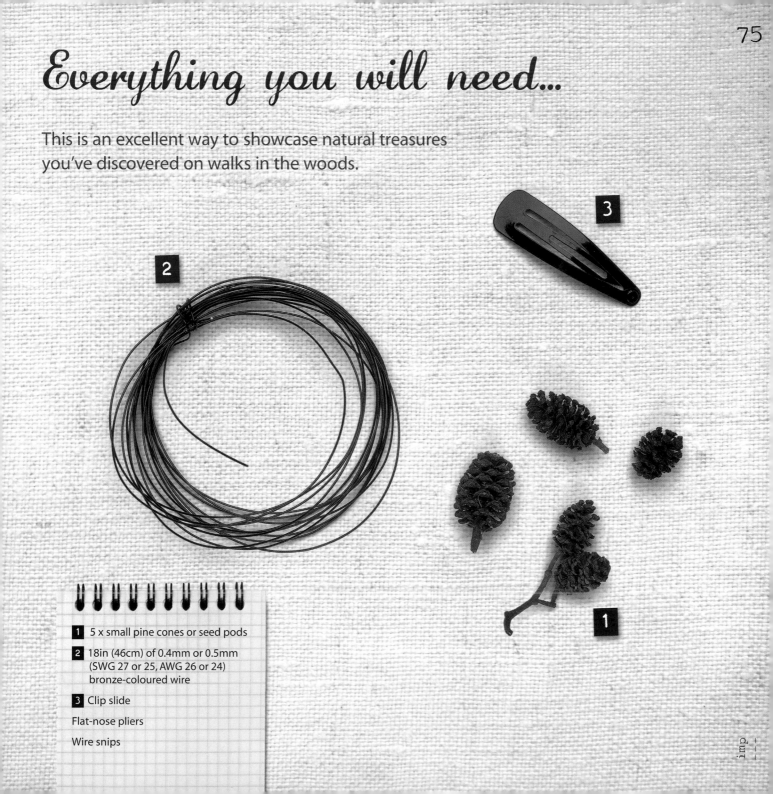

1. 5 x small pine cones or seed pods
2. 18in (46cm) of 0.4mm or 0.5mm (SWG 27 or 25, AWG 26 or 24) bronze-coloured wire
3. Clip slide

Flat-nose pliers

Wire snips

Assembling imp

1 Cut the stalks off your cones with your snips so that you can incorporate them into your twisted wirework more easily.

2 Bend the wire in half and wrap the middle of it tightly around one of the cones. Twist the wire together to create a stem about ½ in (13mm) long. Take the two ends of wire out to the sides (see page 18).

3 On one arm add another cone about ½ in (13mm) from the initial stem as before, then twist the wire until the branch reaches the central trunk.

4 Add another cone onto the other arm of wire in the same way. Twist the two arms of wire together to continue the central trunk down, then take one end of wire out to the side, twist on another cone and create another branch.

5 Add the fifth cone in the same way. Twist the two ends of wire together for about 4in (10cm).

6 Wrap this twisted trunk around the wider end of the slide on both sides of the central bar. Snip any rough edges of wire off, and squeeze the wrapped wire firmly onto the slide with the pliers so it doesn't wobble about (see page 27).

A CLUSTER OF THESE CONE BRANCHES LOOKS LOVELY ON THE SIDE OF A HEADBAND OR ON A COMB.

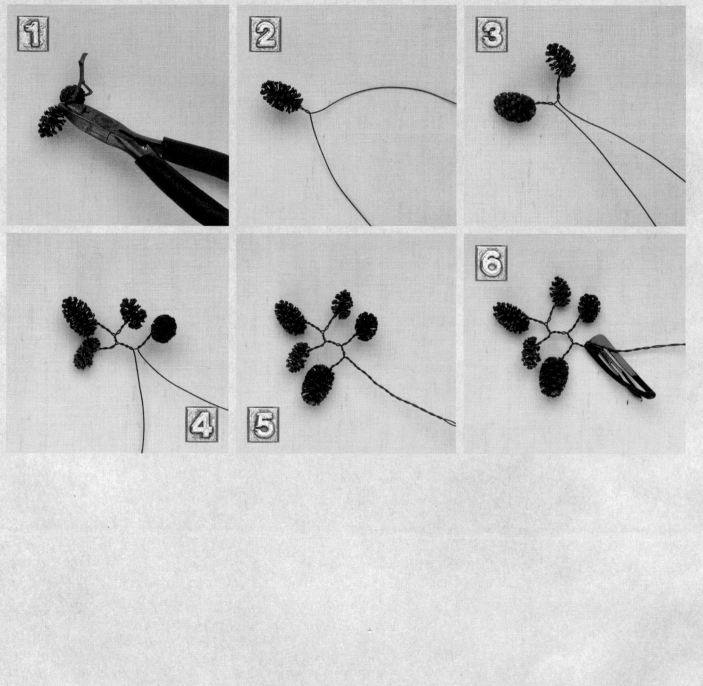

titania

This twig tiara has a pretty,
fairytale look that lends a dreamy,
Art-Nouveau feel to any outfit.

Everything you will need...

This uses a free-form wirework technique that is great for harnessing found materials, allowing you to make natural things into pretty jewellery.

1

x5

2

3

x10–15

1 5 x freshly cut thin twigs

2 5ft (1.5m) of 0.6mm (SWG 24, AWG 23) silver-plated wire

3 10–15 x 6mm beads

Wire snips

Flat-nose pliers

Assembling titania

1 Using your snips, cut the leaves and buds off the twigs and trim the twigs to about 8in (20cm) long.

2 Cut a length of wire about 20in (50cm) long and use this to bind your twigs together about ³/₄in (2cm) from one end. You'll probably need to wrap the wire around the twigs about five times as tightly as possible.

3 Make a small loop in the wire with your pliers and wrap the wire back around on itself.

4 Gently weave the twigs in and out of each other using a loose plaiting technique to create a lattice effect.

5 Smooth the wire into a nice curve with your thumb and forefinger near to where you bound the twigs together. Then thread a bead onto the wire and hold it in place by doing a half-wrap around it (see page 22).

6 Ease the wire into a curve again, then wrap it around one of the twigs. Continue the curve (upwards or downwards) and attach another bead in the same way. Wrap the wire around a different twig each time; you're aiming to keep the lattice effect with space between the twigs and wirework.

7 Continue along the twigs in the same way until you reach the end where you need to bind the other end of the twigs together, as you did at the start. Trim the ends of the twigs if necessary and add a loop in the same way as you did at the other end.

8 Work your way back along the twigs in the opposite direction, attaching beads and wiring onto the twigs as before. If you run out of wire, just wrap the end onto the twigs, cut another 20in (50cm) length and join it back onto the tiara by wrapping it around a couple of times. When you reach the other end, wrap the wire around a couple of times and leave any extra wire attached.

9 Ease the tiara round into a horseshoe shape, then use the excess wire to pull the ends together in an arch shape. Allow about 24–48 hours for the headdress to 'dry' into shape. When it has, snip off the excess wire and squeeze the tail end into place with the pliers. Attach the headdress to your hair using hair grips pushed through the loops and you're all set to become a woodland nymph!

USE FRESHLY CUT TWIGS SO THAT THEY ARE STILL GREEN AND BENDY.

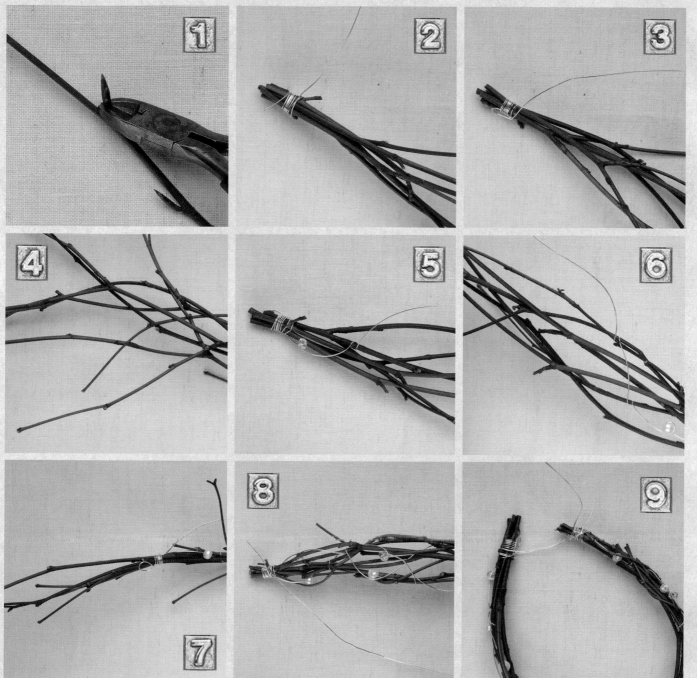

chestnut

This quirky hair
elastic adds seasonal
fun to your ponytail.

Everything you will need...

With this simple but eye-catching natural decoration you're guaranteed to turn heads.

1 3 x horse chestnut seeds or other woodland treasure

2 18in (46cm) of 0.4mm (SWG 27, AWG 26) black wire

3 Hair elastic (with metal join)

Rotary power tool or hand drill with $\frac{1}{8}$in (3mm) drill bit

Masking tape (optional)

Wire snips

Flat-nose pliers

Scissors

chestnut

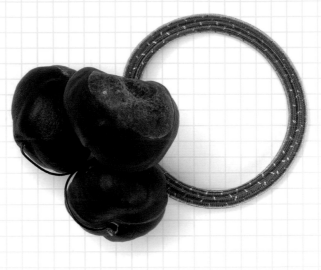

Assembling chestnut

1 Carefully drill a hole through the centre of each chestnut. You can tape the chestnut to your workbench to keep it steady.

2 Take the length of wire and thread one of the chestnuts onto it. Fold the wire at its mid point and position the chestnut there.

3 Twist the wire together under the chestnut three times.

4 Thread another chestnut onto one of the wire ends, fold the wire underneath it and twist it to secure the second chestnut next to the first.

5 Add the third chestnut to the wire in the same way.

6 Twist the ends of the wire together to create a stalk about 4in (10cm) long and wrap it four or five times around the metal join of the hair elastic. Snip off any extra wire and squeeze the wrapped wire firmly into place with the pliers (see page 27) so it doesn't wobble.

INSTEAD OF CHESTNUTS YOU COULD USE

SLICES OF BRANCHES OR PINE CONES.

faerie

With this headband
you'll be queen of
the enchanted forest.

Everything you will need...

This looks ethereal on crazy, curly hair. Lie down in the leaves and lichen wearing your crocheted faerie headband and let the daydreams begin.

3 x20–25

1. 36in (91cm) of 0.3mm or 0.4mm (SWG 30 or 27, AWG 29 or 26) silver-plated wire

2. A couple of handfuls of moss, lichen or leaves

3. 20–25 x crystals or beads

4. Tiara base

Large crochet hook

Flat-nose pliers

Wire snips

faerie

Assembling faerie

1 Cut a 12in (30cm) length of the wire. Make a loop in the end by just twisting the end around itself, then put your crochet hook through it from front to back.

2 Crochet a chain of loose loops about 8in (20cm) long (see page 20).

3 When you're ready to go back the other way and crochet into the first chain, hold the moss or lichen in small pieces behind the chain and crochet through it. Push the hook through the chain and then the lichen before you bring the wire around the hook. Continue to the other end.

4 You'll probably run out of wire by the time you get to the other end, so finish it off by pulling the wire through the last loop to tie a knot. Cut another 12in (30cm) length of wire and add it on by wrapping it through the last loop a couple of times.

5 Thread your beads onto the wire and make a little loop at the end of the wire so they don't all fall off.

6 Crochet into the second row of chain and lichen, adding beads as you go – just push each bead into place before you wrap the wire around the hook.

7 When you get to the other end, tie off the wire as before and snip off any excess wire. Then just shape your work a bit by pressing the beads to the front, maybe stretching out and flattening it a bit.

8 Wrap a 10in (25cm) length of wire 1$\frac{1}{2}$in (38mm) from the bottom of the tiara base (stretched into a horseshoe shape) and hold the crocheted piece across the base. Stitch through the crochet with the wire so it sits snugly across the base. When you get to the other end, wrap the wire around the base about five times to make it really firm. Snip off the excess wire, squeeze the ends flat with the pliers (see page 27) and you're done.

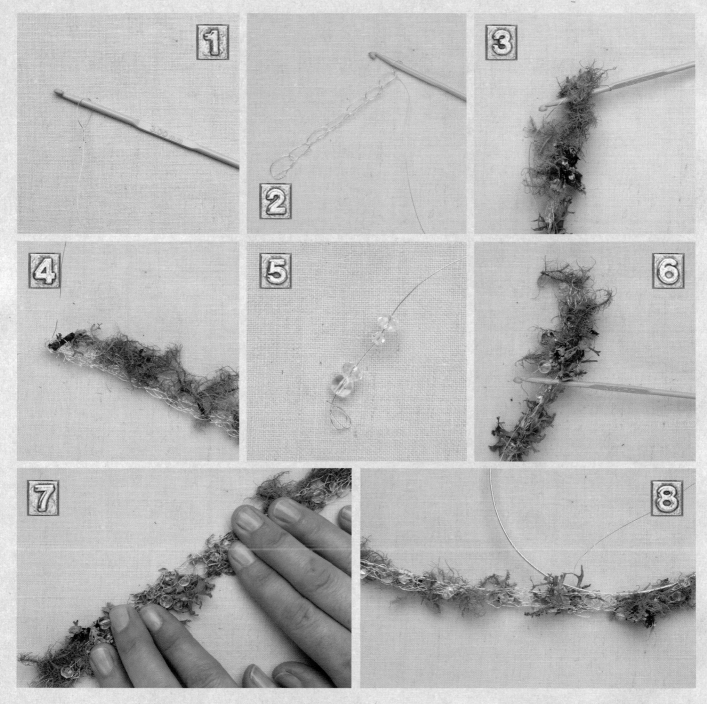

geisha

This oh-so-pretty comb has a
delicate Japanese feel to it.

Everything you will need...

This pretty comb takes its inspiration from Japanese cherry blossom. Try combining the twigs in different ways to see what gorgeous, delicate shapes you can create.

1 5 x small green twigs (freshly cut or kept in water)

2 Plain hair comb

3 11–16 x crystal beads

4 18–30 x pearls

5 18in (46cm) of 0.6mm (SWG 24, AWG 23) silver-plated wire

6 24in (61cm) of 0.4mm (SWG 27, AWG 26) silver-plated wire

Wire snips

Flat-nose pliers

4 x18–30   **3** x11–16

geisha

Assembling geisha

1 Trim the leaves and buds off the twigs.

2 Cut about 10in (25cm) of the 0.6mm wire. Hold the twigs horizontally along the top of the comb and firmly bind them together and around the last few prongs of the comb.

3 Curve the wire upwards, thread on a crystal and secure with a half-wrap (see page 22).

4 Continue along the comb in this way, separating the twigs to wrap the wire around one once and adding a crystal before continuing on. When you reach the other end of the comb, turn around and work back adding crystals and separating twigs as you go. Attach more wire around the comb and twigs as needed. When you get back to your starting point, wrap the remaining wire around the twigs and snip off any excess. Squeeze the wire with pliers to finish off (see page 27).

5 To make a blossom, cut 8in (20cm) of the 0.4mm wire and thread on a small pearl to 3in (7.5cm) from the other end. Do a half-wrap, then thread another pearl on right next to the first one and do another half-wrap. Add six in this way to create a neat circle. Twist the ends of the wires together once or twice underneath your circle.

6 Thread a crystal onto one end of the wire and position it over the front of the bead flower. Take the wire through to the back of the flower and twist the two wire ends together to form a stalk.

7 Decide where you'd like your flower to sit on the comb, then wrap it around the twigs or wire to hold it in position. Make two to four more blossoms and attach them in the same way on the comb. Snip off the excess wire, squeeze in any ends with the pliers (see page 27) and your sweet blossom comb is finished.

TRY DANGLING CHAINS OR LINKED BEADS OFF THE END OF THE TWIGS TO MAKE THE COMB LOOK EVEN MORE GEISHA-STYLE.

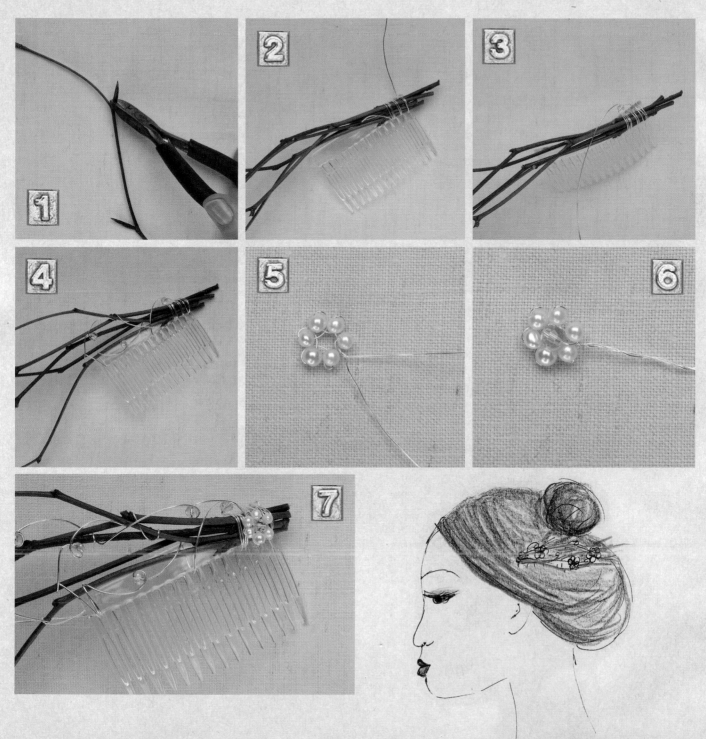

vintage

bling

Create maximum impact
with this sparkly slide.

Everything you will need...

Make a feature of an odd earring you might have lying about. Combine it with an eclectic mix of beads and crystals to end up with a striking, sparkly hair slide.

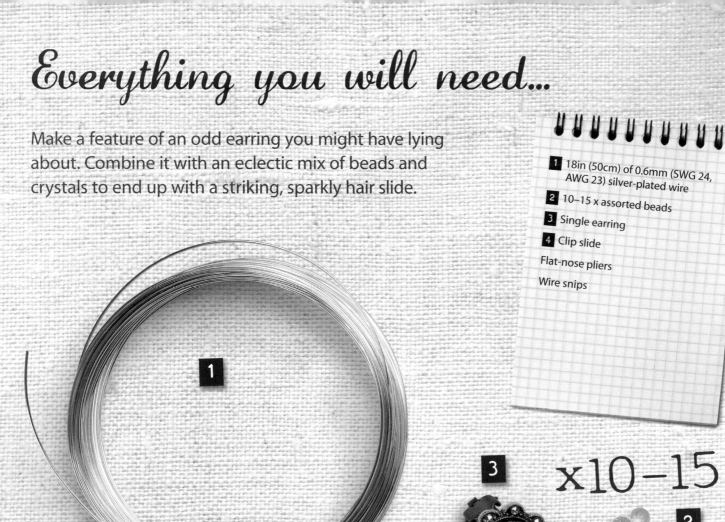

1 18in (50cm) of 0.6mm (SWG 24, AWG 23) silver-plated wire

2 10–15 x assorted beads

3 Single earring

4 Clip slide

Flat-nose pliers

Wire snips

x10–15

Assembling bling

1 Thread a bead onto the length of wire and push it down to around 3in (7.5cm) from the other end.

2 Loop the wire around the bead, from hole to hole in a half-wrap so that the bead is held in place (see page 22).

3 Thread another bead onto the end of the wire not used for wrapping and push it down next to the first one, then wrap it in the same way as before. Add a few more in this way, working in a roughly circular shape.

4 Ease the clasp from the back of your earring using the pliers.

5 Thread the earring onto the wire after the bead cluster.

6 Add more beads around the earring in the same way as you did in step 3. You are aiming for a tight, spherical cluster of beads.

7 When you're happy with the shape of the cluster, squeeze the design a bit tighter with your pliers and then thread the wire through the design a couple of times to hold it together.

8 Attach the cluster to the slide by threading the excess wire through the wide end a few times and wrapping it around the slide. Snip off any excess wire, and you're finished!

IF YOU DON'T HAVE AN OLD EARRING THEN A SMALL BROOCH WILL WORK JUST AS WELL FOR MAKING THIS SLIDE.

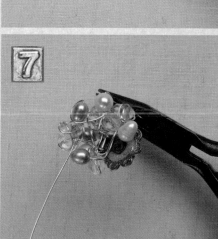

carmen

Bring old brooches back to life as a stunning theatrical headdress.

Everything you will need...

This glamorous headdress is perfect for sophisticated brides or to wear on a special night out. Three vintage brooches clustered together create a luxurious shape guaranteed to be unique.

1 Piece of lace about 2¹⁄₂ x 4in (10 x 6cm)

2 Tiara base

3 3 x old brooches

4 30–35 x assorted beads and crystals

5 2ft (70cm) of 0.6mm (SWG 24, AWG 23) gold-plated wire

6 2ft (70cm) ribbon to match your hair colour

Small sharp scissors

Wire snips

Needle or nail file

Flat-nose pliers

PVA glue

x30–35

Assembling carmen

1 Soak the lace in some watered-down PVA glue in a plastic container. Remove from the glue and leave to dry on a plastic bag overnight (see page 23). Trim the lace to the shape you want.

2 Shape the tiara base by bending both ends outwards, so the base has a horseshoe rather than a round shape, then wrap the end of a 10in (25cm) length of the wire around the base three times, about 2in (5cm) from the tiara base end.

3 Thread a pearl or crystal onto the wire and push it down so that it is about ½–¾in (1–2cm) away from the base. Take the wire around the bead from one hole to the other so that the bead is firmly held in a half-wrap (see page 22). Then wrap the wire once around the tiara base about 1in (2.5cm) along.

4 Hold the piece of lace against the front of the tiara base, next to the first bead. Pass the wire through the lace to hold it in place. Smooth the wire in a nice curve with your thumb and forefinger and then thread on another bead. Wrap this in a half-wrap as before. Take the wire through the lace and wrap around the tiara base.

5 Work your way along the tiara base, attaching beads approximately every 1in (2.5cm) in the same way. Every now and then take the wire around the bead in the opposite direction so that it sits on the other side of the curve of the wire. If you want the headdress to be asymmetric, stop about 4in (10cm) from the other end; if you want the design to go right across your head, keep going until you are 2in (5cm) from the end.

6 Wrap the wire around the base three times, then go back over the lace creating a second row. Build up the design on both sides of the band. When you reach the end of the wire, wrap it around the base three times and attach the remaining wire as before.

7 Prepare your brooches by removing the pins. Using your snips, cut through the pin close to the hinge in a careful, controlled way so the pin doesn't fly off. Gently snip the pin base in one direction, then the other. If it's a bit tough, just take your time and keep snipping round in different directions. Old base metals are normally quite soft and it should come away quite easily. File down any rough edges that are left.

8 Attach another piece of wire about 12in (30cm) long at the start again. Hold the first brooch in your chosen position, then thread the wire through a hole on the brooch and wrap it around the tiara base. Next, thread the wire through the brooch at the other end, and wrap around the base so that the brooch is held very firmly in place. Attach the other two brooches in their positions in the same way. Snip off the tail end of wire and squeeze the end flat with the pliers (see page 27).

9 File off any rough edges so that the inside feels smooth. Tie the ribbon around one end of the tiara base, then wind it around the base to completely cover it. Tie a knot when you get to the other end of the tiara base, then tuck the end of ribbon in and secure with a blob of glue (see page 26).

TRY USING CRYSTALS FROM BROKEN-UP VINTAGE NECKLACES AS THE COLOURS ARE MORE SUBTLE AND IN KEEPING WITH THIS RETRO DESIGN.

clarice

Combine an old brooch with fabric foliage for an elegant decoration.

Everything you will need...

A vintage-style comb is a lovely way to give your hair a subtle bit of vintage glamour. Or make two to embellish a 1940s-style victory roll.

1

2

5

4

3

x15–20

1 24in (60cm) of 0.6mm (SWG 24, AWG 23) silver-plated wire

2 Plain hair comb

3 15–20 x beads

4 Antique brooch (with a few open spaces)

5 Artificial leaf sprayed silver

Wire snips

Small metal file or nail file

Flat-nose pliers

clarice

Assembling clarice

1 Wrap one end of the piece of wire around the top of the comb between the last two prongs about three times.

2 Choose your first bead and thread it onto the free end of the wire. Move it down the wire until it is about ½in (1cm) from the comb and then wrap the wire around the bead, from one hole to the other, to hold the bead in place (see page 22).

3 Using your thumb and forefinger, smooth the wire into a curve and then add your next bead. Wrap the wire around it again from one hole to the other to hold it in place, then wrap the wire once around the comb a couple of prongs along to make your desired curved shape.

4 Work your way along the top of the comb in this way, adding more beads and attaching the wire to the top of the comb a couple of times. Then work your way back to where you started in the same way. To make the decoration look less uniform, try occasionally curving the wire upwards instead of down before you attach the next bead, so that it sits on the other side of the wire.

5 Prepare your brooch by snipping the pin off the back. Using your snips, cut through the pin close to the hinge in a careful, controlled way so the pin doesn't fly off. Gently snip the pin base in one direction, then the other. If it's a bit tough, just take your time and keep snipping round in different directions. File the sharp edge left behind to make it smooth.

6 Attach the brooch to the end of your comb simply by finding a hole in the brooch structure, threading the wire through and wrapping it around the comb (in two places ideally).

7 Attach the artificial leaf behind the brooch by pushing the wire gently through the leaf or stalk and moving it down into place.

8 Carry on adding beads to your design in a similar way as before. To build the design upwards, away from the comb, wrap the wire around the initial wirework instead of the comb.

9 When you get to the other end of the comb, wrap the remaining wire around the last prong three times to secure it, squeezing it with your pliers to make sure it's nice and tight (see page 27). Snip any excess wire off, then style your hair and try it on!

WHEN YOU REMOVE THE BACK OF THE BROOCH, TRY NOT TO PULL IT BACK AND FORTH TOO MUCH AS YOU CAN END UP LOOSENING STONES.

INSTEAD OF BEADS TRY USING SPARKLY VINTAGE CRYSTALS OR CUT-UP PIECES OF DIAMANTE OR SEMI-PRECIOUS STONES.

Hair accessories

flapper

Get ready to do the
Charleston with this
jazz-age headdress.

Everything you will need...

A Deco look is captured with this headdress, which is gorgeous worn forward on the forehead, particularly with a lovely swinging hairdo or fluffy curly bob.

1. 3ft 3in (1m) of 0.6mm (SWG 24, AWG 23) silver-plated wire
2. Tiara base
3. 30 x assorted vintage beads and pearls
4. 2ft (70cm) fine chain
5. Vintage brooch

Wire snips

Flat-nose pliers

Nail or needle file

Superglue

Iron

x30

Assembling flapper

1 Cut a length of wire 16in (40cm) long and at its middle point, wrap it three times around the tiara base about 2in (5cm) from one end.

2 Thread about 8 beads onto one of the loose wire ends, then carefully curve the wire over the headdress following the shape of the tiara base. This wire should sit to one side of the base; wrap the wire around the base 2in (5cm) from the other end.

3 Add 8 or 9 beads to the other long end of wire, ease it to the other side of the band and wrap it at the same point as before: don't cut off the excess wire yet as you can use it to attach the brooch and chain.

4 Attach another 16in (40cm) long piece of wire to the tiara, starting on the opposite end to before. Add the rest of the beads as before, dividing them unequally between the two ends of wire. Ease the wires over to the other side of the headdress so that they sit either side of the first bead-laden lengths of wire. Wrap these at the opposite side as before.

5 Snip three varied lengths of chain for each side and thread them onto one of the loose ends of wire. Wrap the wire around the base to hold them in place. On one side, trim the second wire neatly and squeeze with the pliers (see page 27).

6 Prepare your vintage brooch by carefully cutting off the pin and filing down any sharp edges. Firmly wire the brooch into your chosen position using the remaining end of wire. Trim off any excess wire and squeeze the end flat with the pliers.

7 To finish off, carefully dot glue at random points on the long pieces of wire and gently push the beads into place. Leave the headdress upright so that the glue can dry while you fix your cocktail.

FOR A SLINKY BRIDAL LOOK ATTACH NET UNDER THE BROOCH AND TAKE IT ACROSS THE HEAD TO THE OTHER SIDE SO IT SITS SNUGLY OVER A SHINY BOB.

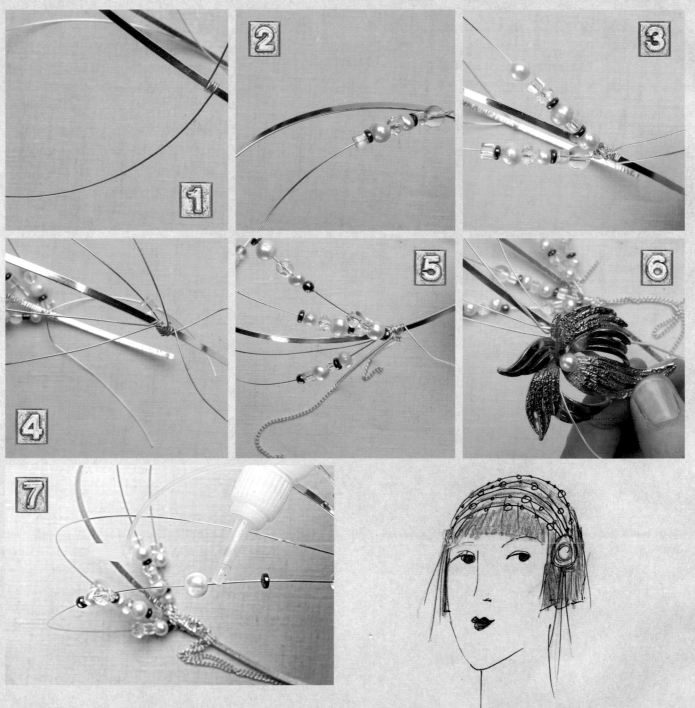

twinkle

Add a dash of sparkle
to your look with this
delicate, pretty tiara.

Everything you will need...

Get a load of mileage out of a 1950s sparkly crystal necklace or old pearls by twisting the beads into a dreamy tiara that can be worn many different ways.

2

3

1 50–70 x different-sized vintage pearls and crystals

2 6ft 6in (2m) of 0.3mm or 0.4mm (SWG 30 or 27, AWG 29 or 26) silver-plated wire

3 Tiara base

Flat-nose pliers

Wire snips

1

x50–70

twinkle

Assembling twinkle

1 If you're using an old necklace, break it up with your pliers. Cut about 12in (30cm) of the wire, thread on your first pearl and push it to the middle point of the wire. Bring both pieces of wire together underneath the bead and then twist the bead with your finger and thumb so that the ends of wire twist together for about 1in (2.5cm).

2 Next, thread a pearl onto one of the ends of wire, fold it at a point about $^1/_2$in (13mm) from the centre trunk and twist the pearl so that the wire forms a branch that joins the main trunk (see page 18). Do the same with a pearl on the other wire end.

3 Twist the two wire ends together to continue the trunk downwards, then take the ends out to each side again. This time add two pearls at separate points on each branch, twisting after each pearl.

4 Continue the trunk down a few twists, then add another branch with two pearls on the other side.

5 Add another pair of branches. Twist the two ends together a bit before making the opposite branch to make it look less regular and more natural. When you're happy with the pearls on your branch, continue twisting the two ends of wire together to create a stalk that you can use to attach it to the tiara.

6 Make five 'trees' in this way and vary it as much as you like. You can add two beads at separate points of the branch or add several small beads in one loop at the top, as shown here.

7 Once you've made your trees, lay them out to plan how you'd like them to sit on the tiara. You could aim for quite a traditional shape with the design rising in the middle, or arrange them all at the same height for a more 1950s retro look.

8 Pull the ends of the tiara base outwards to create a horseshoe shape that's more comfortable to wear. Attach the middle branch first by wrapping it at least three times around the middle point of the tiara base, either side of the branch 'stem'. Work from the middle outwards and attach the other branches firmly in the same way. Squeeze any loose ends flat with the pliers (see page 27), and you're done!

THE TIARA LOOKS BEST IF YOU VARY THE BRANCHES AND TREES. WHEN YOU'VE ATTACHED ALL THE WIRE BRANCHES BEND AND CRUSH THEM A BIT TO MAKE THEM LOOK LESS REGIMENTED.

WRAP SOFT ORGANZA RIBBON ALONG THE TIARA BASE BETWEEN AND OVER THE WRAPPED WIRE FOR A NEAT FINISH AND TO TONE IN WITH YOUR HAIR (SEE PAGE 26).

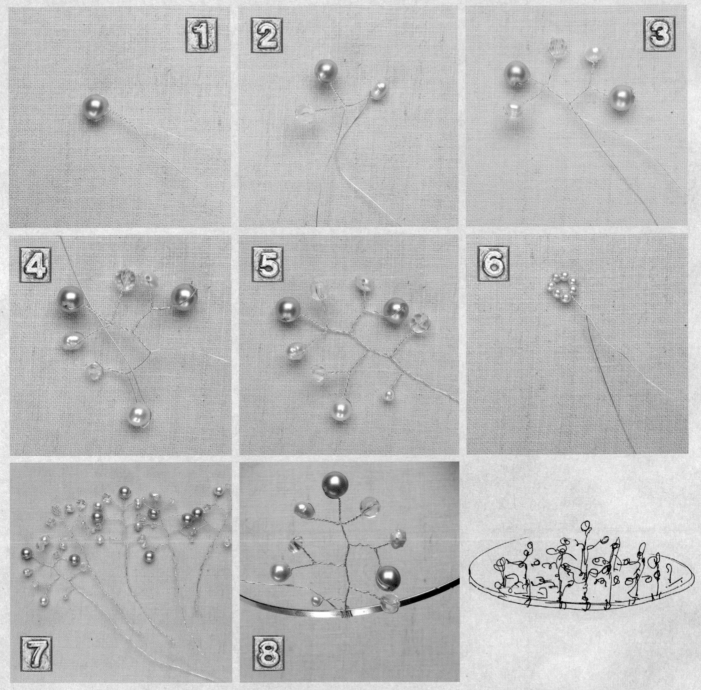

resources

BOOKS

MATERIALS AND INSPIRATION

Jewellery from Natural Materials
by Beth Legg (A&C Black
Publishers, 2008)

Sustainable Jewellery by Julia
Manheim (A&C Black
Publishers, 2009)

*Textile Techniques in Metal:
For Jewelers, Textile Artists
& Sculptors*
by Arline M Fisch
(Lark Books, 2001)

Adorn: New Jewellery
by Amanda Mansell (Laurence
King, 2008)

Fashion Drawing in Vogue
by William Packer and David
Hockney (Thames and Hudson,
2010)

Pattern by Orla Kiely
(Conran Octopus, 2010)

AUSTRALIA
Beads Online
PO Box 160
Tweed Heads
New South Wales 2487
www.beadsonline.com.au

CHINA
Gets.cn
12A-09 Room
Building 1
No 21 Shun san tiao
Song Zhuang Road
Fengtai Zone
Beijing
Tel: +86 10 6763 9955
www.gets.cn

Panda Hall
5th Floor East
25 Building
Central District of High-tech
Industrial Park
Shen Zhen City
Guang Dong Province
Tel: +86 755 2697 2706
www.pandahall.com

USA
BlueMud
17837 1st Avenue South PMB
#513
Seattle
Washington 98148
www.bluemud.com

Bocage
PO Box 5662
Santa Barbara
California 93150-5662
www.bocagenewyork.com

D & I Beads
5350 W. Bell Rd #136
Glendale
Arizona 85308
Tel: +1 602-564-2900
www.dibeads.com

Fire Mountain Gems and Beads
One Fire Mountain Way
Grants Pass
Oregon 97526-2373
Tel: +1 800-355-2137
www.firemountaingems.com

MKBeads
618 SW 3rd Street #150
Cape Coral
Florida 33991
Tel: +1 239-634-2232
Email: sales@mkbeads.com
www.mkbeads.com

Ruby Lane
381 Bush Street
Suite 400
San Francisco
California 94104
Tel: +1 415-362-7611
http://jewelry.rubylane.com

Hair accessories

UK

Abby's Attic
Market House
Market Street
St Austell
Cornwall
PL25 5QB

Big Bad Beads
The Old Sunday School
Cape Cornwall Street
St Just
Cornwall
TR19 7JZ
info@bigbadbeads.co.uk
www.bigbadbeads.co.uk

Bijoux Beads
9 Berwick Courtyard
Berwick St Leonard
Salisbury
Wiltshire
SP3 5UA
Tel: +44 (0)1747 820562
www.bijouxbeads.co.uk

Country Baskets
Ardsley Mills
Bradford Road
East Ardsley
Leeds
WF3 2DW
Tel: +44 (0)113 218 9090
www.countrybaskets.co.uk

Fred Aldous
37 Lever Street
Manchester
M1 1LW
support@fredaldous.zendesk.com
Tel: +44 (0)161 236 4224
www.fredaldous.co.uk

Homecrafts Direct
Hamilton House
Mountain Road
Leicester
LE4 9HQ
Tel: +44 (0)116 269 7733
www.homecrafts.co.uk

Jewellery Shed
Unit 5B
Mullacott Cross Industrial Estate
Ilfracombe
Devon
EX34 8PL
Tel: +44 (0)843 2894080
www.jewelleryshed.co.uk

JillyBeads
1 Anstable Road
Morecambe
LA4 6TG
Tel: +44 (0)1524 412728
Email: info@jillybeads.co.uk
www.jillybeads.co.uk

MacCulloch & Wallis
25-26 Dering Street
London
W1S 1AT
Tel: +44 (0)20 7629 0311
www.macculloch-wallis.co.uk

P J Beads
583C Liverpool Road
Southport
PR8 3LU
Tel: +44 (0)1704 575461
Email: info@beads.co.uk
www.beads.co.uk

Truro Fabrics
Lemon Quay
Truro
Cornwall
TR1 2LW
Tel: +44 (0)1872 222130
www.trurofabrics.com

Wires.co.uk
Unit 3 Zone A
Chelmsford Road Industrial Estate
Great Dunmow
Essex
CM6 1HD
Tel: +44 (0)1371 238013
www.wires.co.uk

GENERAL

Vintage materials can be sourced from online auction sites such as www.ebay.co.uk and www.ebay.com.

Antique fairs, markets, second-hand shops and charity stores are all good sources of fabrics, buttons and jewellery.

about the author

Sarah Drew has been making strange things out of found materials since she was about six. She used to raid her father's garage for suitable bolts and hinges to make into *Star Trek* gadgets. Once she made a wig out of a holey orange net bag and loads of brown wool. She doesn't know why; it took ages. Sarah has been running her jewellery business since 2000, when she returned to the UK after travelling round Australia. Having sold jewellery to subsidize the trip, Sarah started making tiaras and beaded jewellery using vintage brooches and beads when she returned home to York. Since moving to Cornwall in 2006, she's had the chance to collect lovely weathered beach plastic, sea string, sea glass and driftwood from local beaches to use in her collections. Sarah also teaches classes on making recycled jewellery and she likes to collect the found materials with people for them to use in creating their jewellery.

Sarah lives in St Austell, Cornwall with her husband, two sons and Rosie the mad dog. Her boys collect odd things for her to use in her jewellery – anybody fancy a crab claw necklace? – and keep her quite busy. She enjoys retreating to her little shop and workspace for a bit of peace, girly prettiness and proper coffee. *www.sarahdrew.com*

Sarah would like to dedicate this book to her boys, Tom, Joseph and Alfie.

index

Project names are given in italics

To order a book, or to request
a catalogue, contact:

GMC Publications Ltd
Castle Place,
166 High Street,
Lewes,
East Sussex,
BN7 1XU
United Kingdom

Tel: +44 (0)1273 488005

www.gmcbooks.com